FIRE DOGS

by Donna Latham

Consultant: Wilma Melville, Founder
National Disaster Search Dog Foundation

New York, New York

Special thanks to Wilma Melville who founded the:
National Disaster Search Dog Foundation
206 N. Signal Street, Suite R
Ojai, CA 93023
(888) 4K9-HERO
www.SearchDogFoundation.org

The Search Dog Foundation is a not-for-profit organization that rescues dogs, gives them professional training, and partners them with firefighters to find people buried alive in disasters. They produce the most highly trained search dogs in the nation.

Original design and production by Dawn Beard Creative and Octavo Design and Production, Inc.

Credits

Cover, Front(left), Dennis Light / Light Photographic, (top right), Tim Snopek Photography / timsnopek.com; (center right), John Gurzinski / Las Vegas Review Journal; (bottom right), Dennis Light / Light Photographic; Back (top), Tim Snopek Photography / timsnopek.com; (center), John Gurzinski / Las Vegas Review Journal; (bottom), Dennis Light / Light Photographic. Title page, Dennis Light / Light Photographic. Page 3, Chris Mickal / New Orleans Fire Department Photo Unit; 4–5, Tim Snopek Photography / timsnopek.com; 6, Dennis Light / Light Photographic; 7, AP / Wide World Photos; 8–9, courtesy, Val Ansett, NSW Fire Brigades, Australia; 9, Corbis; 10, Chris Mickal / New Orleans Fire Department Photo Unit; 11, AP / Wide World Photos; 12–13, Alex Wong / Getty Images; 14, AP / Wide World Photos; 15, Andre Jansen; 16–17(both), Dennis Light / Light Photographic; 18–19, John Gurzinski / Las Vegas Review Journal; 20, Fire Logic Fire Investigators; 21, AP / Wide World Photos; 22–23, Kristen Schmid / The State Journal-Register; 24–25, Michael Heller / 911 Pictures; 25, Fire Logic Fire Investigators; 26–27, Dennis Light / Light Photographic; 28, Dan Dempster / Dembinsky Photo Associates; 29(top), Fotosearch.com; 29(center), Alamy Images; 29(bottom), Fotosearch.com.

Library of Congress Cataloging-in-Publication Data

Latham, Donna.
Fire dogs / by Donna Latham.
  p. cm.—(Dog heroes)
Includes bibliographical references and index.
ISBN 1-59716-141-1 (library binding)—ISBN 1-59716-143-8 (pbk.)
1. Arson investigation—Juvenile literature. 2. Firehouse dogs—Juvenile literature. I. Title.
II. Series.

HV8079.A7L38 2006
363.25'964—dc22

2005009083

For more information, write to Bearport Publishing Company, Inc., 101 Fifth Avenue, Suite 6R, New York, New York 10003. Printed in the United States of America.

3 4 5 6 7 8 9 10

Table of Contents

Fire!

From a safe distance, Michael and Carli stared at the raging fire. Already it had **devoured** the garage behind their house.

Michael told **Investigator** Scott Tebo (TEE-bo) about a small car accident he'd had earlier. The driver of the other car had seemed angry.

"He must have followed me home," said Michael. "Carli and I heard a *boom*! I looked outside and saw the guy running near our garage. Then the garage burst into flames."

Scott decided to begin his investigation right away. First, however, he went to his car and opened the door. His yellow Labrador retriever, Blaze, quickly jumped out.

An arson investigator works to find the origin, or starting point, of a fire. He or she also tries to find out what caused the fire.

Firefighters work hard to put out flames.

An Arson Dog

Blaze moved through the crowd of people watching the fire. Even though they reached out to pet her, Blaze knew her job. She quickly began to sniff around.

Blaze would help Scott find the cause of the fire. Had it been started by accident, or was it set on purpose?

Blaze and Arson Investigator Scott Tebo

People who use fire to destroy property are guilty of a crime called arson. Arsonists often use **accelerants** to start fires or make them spread more quickly. Arson dogs such as Blaze can smell accelerants. They can often find the exact spot where a fire began.

The accelerants that arsonists most often use, such as gasoline and kerosene, are made from oil.

Arson dogs sniff for small amounts of accelerants left after a fire. Dogs usually do not visit a fire scene until the entire area has cooled.

Super Sniffers

Arson is a tough crime to solve. Much of the **evidence** goes up in flames. Also, to put out a fire, huge amounts of water have to be used. The water **dilutes** accelerants, however, and washes away important clues about what started the fire.

Arson dog Ellie

"That's when Blaze really has to work to pick up the **scent**," says Scott.

A dog's sense of smell is 1,000 times sharper than a person's. Arson dogs can even smell tiny amounts of accelerants that have been watered down. Blaze can pick up the scent of 16 different kinds of these liquids.

Dogs have special sniffing cells to help them get a good whiff of a scent.

Dogs have been trained to sniff out missing people, find hidden bombs, and even detect microscopic cancer cells by sniffing a person's skin.

The First Arson Dog

Dogs are known as "man's best friend." Because they are loyal, **alert**, and intelligent, dogs make great **companions**. These same qualities—plus their sniffing skills—are the reasons that dogs are valuable in helping arson investigators.

Roxy works for the New Orleans Fire Department. Roxy follows her nose to find evidence.

The first arson dog was Mattie, a black Labrador retriever. She was a gift from the Guide Dog Foundation to the Connecticut State Police (CSP).

The CSP wanted to learn if dogs could be used in arson investigations. Mattie's training began on May 1, 1986. Within a year, the CSP knew that the project was a success. Mattie had learned to sniff out 17 accelerants.

A Connecticut police officer helps his partner on an obstacle course.

Today, there are about 200 arson dogs in the United States.

Eager to Please

Labrador retrievers are playful, energetic, and intelligent. They have calm natures and good **temperaments**.

Labs were first **bred** as hunting dogs. They are still used to hunt game birds and to retrieve, or get and bring back, animals that hunters shoot. Labs can retrieve in the water as well as on land. They can also squeeze into tight places that people can't fit into.

Arson dogs work for about 20 minutes at a time. Then they rest for a while before going back to work.

An arson dog lives with his or her **handler**. When not on the trail of a crime, the dog enjoys family life.

These qualities make Labs a perfect **breed** for arson work. They have the spirit, strength, and sniffing skills needed for the job. They also enjoy nothing more than being with and pleasing their handlers.

Training Together

Arson dogs and their handlers train for their jobs together. Scott and Blaze, for example, trained for six weeks. First, they spent time getting to know each other. They quickly became friends. Then they learned to work as a team.

In Tennessee, Ron Powers works with Kenda to determine the cause of a fire.

Most arson dogs train for five to eight weeks. Training usually takes place seven days a week, for eight hours a day. During this time, dogs learn to recognize the scents of accelerants. Their handlers, meanwhile, learn the **commands** that send the dogs on the trail of these scents. "Check!" and "Work!" are common commands that drive arson dogs into action.

A K-9 arson investigation patch

Arson dogs and their handlers are called K-9 teams. K-9 is a short way to write *canine*, which means "related to dogs."

Food Rewards

During training, dogs go through daily sniffing sessions. They might sniff for accelerants 125 times in a single day.

At the firehouse, Blaze practices finding accelerants.

Dogs are taught to behave in a certain way when they smell an accelerant. This behavior is called an "alert." The dog sits where the scent is found and looks at the handler. The animal doesn't move until the handler responds. By sitting calmly, the dog doesn't disturb important evidence.

When dogs successfully alert, they are rewarded with food. During training, they are fed only after they sniff an accelerant and give an alert.

Some arson dogs, like Blaze, are rewarded with playtime instead of food. Scott and Blaze play catch with tennis balls.

Tested and Ready for Work

Before Scott and Blaze could work at a real fire scene, both had to pass tests. Scott was given a written exam. Blaze took a field test. To prove she knew her stuff, Blaze sniffed out accelerants.

Josie, a Las Vegas fire dog, examines evidence for signs of arson.

To keep working, all K-9 teams must pass tests every year.

On her first day at work, Blaze went with Scott to a **suspicious** house fire. The same home had caught fire two years earlier. Scott dug out places in a room for Blaze to sniff. She sniffed through **debris** and alerted on one area—twice. When objects from the area were sent to a lab, they tested positive for gasoline.

Buried Under Snow

When fire struck a two-family building in Ohio, arson was suspected. Investigator Dennis Cummings and Smoky, his chocolate Lab, sprang into action. Smoky followed his nose through the building's rooms.

A German shepherd arson dog sniffs for clues.

Eager to please, Smoky made four alerts. He touched one spot with his nose. It was a place where a couch had once rested. However, firefighters had taken the couch outside. Now, it was buried under 26 inches (66 cm) of heavy, fresh snow.

Smoky eagerly climbed up a mound of snow. "He alerted us to the couch," Dennis said. Later, tests showed that an accelerant had set the couch on fire.

In minutes, arson dogs can find out whether accelerants were used to start a fire. Without dogs, it sometimes takes people hours or days to learn the same thing.

Arson dog Vadar checks samples from a house fire. The blaze killed a mother and her son.

Personality and Skills

Sometimes, members of an arson team have similar personalities. Tommy Bychowski (buy-CHOW-skee), like his partner Zee, is super enthusiastic about life.

At the Illinois Capitol, Tommy and Zee show a crowd their skills.

When arson dogs find an accelerant, they seem happy and pleased with themselves.

Tommy gets really excited when he talks about Zee's sniffing skills. He calls them "a fantastic tool" and uses a cheeseburger to explain what he means.

"Humans, we just smell the cheeseburger. The dog smells the bun, the meat, the pickles, the lettuce, the ketchup, everything," says Tommy.

Dangers on the Job

K-9 teams tackle dangerous jobs. Scott Tebo checks each fire scene before Blaze is allowed inside. He makes sure an arsonist isn't hiding. He scouts around for glass, nails, and other sharp objects that could cut Blaze's paws.

Burned-out floors are dangerous for arson dogs and their handlers to walk on.

Scott checks to see that no areas of the floors have burned away. The greatest risk to arson dogs—and their handlers—is falling through caved-in floors. Once, at a fire scene, Blaze alerted. She pointed her nose at a spot to show Scott where she smelled an accelerant. Scott, however, couldn't respond. He'd fallen through a floor up to his waist!

Before dogs search a crime scene, trainers do a safety check to make sure nothing on the floor will hurt the dogs' paws.

In the U.S., about 267,000 fires are set by arsonists each year.

"That's the Guy!"

At the fire at Michael and Carli's house, Scott and Blaze moved through the crowd. Suddenly, Michael spotted someone he recognized. He quietly tipped off Scott. "That's the guy I had the crash with!" he whispered.

Scott headed in the man's direction. Just then, Blaze alerted. She was sitting next to the guy Michael had pointed out! Scott pulled the man aside to question him.

Tests done on the man's clothing found gasoline. They proved that Blaze's alert was correct. Today, this arsonist is in jail. Scott and Blaze, a devoted team, continue their important work.

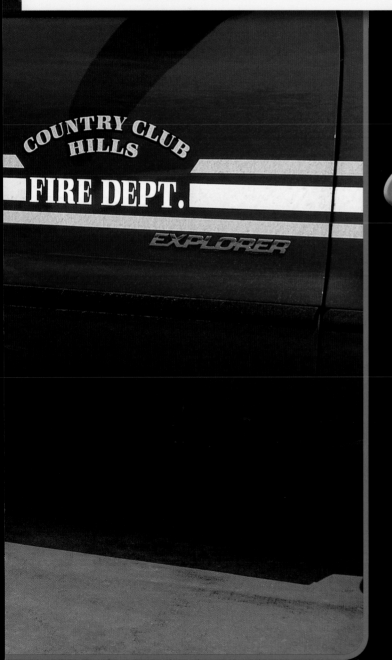

Though very accurate, arson dogs aren't always right. Tests of samples must be done to prove a dog's alert was correct.

Scott and Blaze

Just the Facts

- The first fire dogs were dalmatians (dahl-MAY-shuns). In the 1700s, horses pulled water pumper wagons, used to put out fires. Firefighters noticed that horses were calmer when a dalmatian was with them.

- Arson dogs can be trained to understand commands in more than one language!

- Arson dogs are on call day and night.

- Some arson dogs are bred to be smaller and lighter than Labrador retrievers. The lightweight dogs can move over debris more quickly and easily than heavier dogs.

- Sometimes, handlers put the smell of accelerants on the toys that arson dogs play with.

- Arson results in death, injury, and destroyed property. In 2003, the U.S. Fire Administration reported that 68,000 arson fires were set in buildings and vehicles. These fires caused 305 deaths and lost property totaling $824 million.

yellow Labrador retriever

chocolate Labrador retriever

black Labrador retriever

accelerants (ak-SEL-uh-runts) materials used to start a fire or make a fire stronger

alert (uh-LURT) ready to warn someone of danger; on guard

arson (AR-suhn) the crime of purposely setting a fire

bred (BRED) raised as

breed (BREED) a type of a certain animal

commands (kuh-MANDZ) instructions given to be obeyed; orders

companions (kuhm-PAN-yuhnz) good company and friends

debris (duh-BREE) pieces of broken glass, furniture, and other materials left behind after a fire

devoured (di-VOURD) destroyed; ate hungrily and quickly

dilutes (duh-LUTES) makes weaker because of added water

evidence (EV-uh-duhnss) facts or materials that give proof that a crime has taken place

handler (HAND-lur) a person who trains and works with animals

investigator (in-VESS-tuh-*gay*-tur) someone who tries to find out as much as possible about a crime

scent (SENT) a smell

suspicious (suh-SPISH-uhss) something that looks wrong or false

temperaments (TEM-pur-uh-muhnts) personalities, qualities, or natures

Bibliography

Henrikson, Karen M. "Nikki Visits Crime Prevention Association Meeting in Des Plaines." *Illinois Municipal Review* (May 1996).

New York State Department of State. "Arson Dogs: The State's Fire Investigators." http://www.dos.state.ny.us/kidsroom/firesafe/adogs.html

Reynolds, John. "Arson Dog Zee Shows Her Skills." *Illinois State Register Journal* (Friday, October 10, 2003).

Tebo, Scott, Arson Investigator and K-9 Handler. Country Club Hills, Illinois, Fire Department. Interviews, February 2005.

Read More

Bidner, Jen. *Dog Heroes: Saving Lives and Protecting America.* Guilford, CT.: The Lyons Press (2002).

Clutton-Brock, Juliet. *Dog.* New York: DK Publishing (2004).

Gorrell, Gena K. *Working Like a Dog: The Story of Working Dogs Through History.* Plattsburgh, NY: Tundra Books (2003).

Jackson, Donna M. *Hero Dogs: Courageous Canines in Action.* New York: Megan Tingley Books/Little, Brown (2003).

Tracqui, Valerie. *Face to Face with the Dog: Loyal Companion.* Waterton, MA: Charlesbridge Publishing (2002).

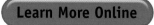
Learn More Online

Visit these Web sites to learn more about fire safety and dogs:

www.akc.org/

www.nfpa.org/sparky/

www.usfa.fema.gov/

Index

About the Author

Donna Latham is a writer and dog lover in the Chicago, Illinois, area. Her Lhasa Apso, Nikki, is one of the canines that *doesn't* want to work for a living.